AUGUSTINE

Confessing Christ

6 studies
for individuals
or groups
with study notes

CLASSICS

Stephen D. Eyre

CAROLYN NYSTROM, Series Editor

InterVarsity Press
Downers Grove, Illinois

InterVarsity Press
P.O. Box 1400, Downers Grove, IL 60515-1426
World Wide Web: www.ivpress.com
E-mail: mail@ivpress.com

InterVarsity Press® is the book-publishing division of InterVarsity Christian Fellowship/USA®, a student movement active on campus at hundreds of universities, colleges and schools of nursing in the United States of America, and a member movement of the International Fellowship of Evangelical Students. For information about local and regional activities, write Public Relations Dept., InterVarsity Christian Fellowship/USA, 6400 Schroeder Rd., P.O. Box 7895, Madison, WI 53707-7895, or visit the IVCF website at <www.ivcf.org>.

Cover and interior illustrations: Roberta Polfus

ISBN 0-8308-2081-7

Printed in the United States of America ∞

P	18	17	16	15	14	13	12	11	10	9	8	7	6	5	4	3	2	1
Y	16	15	14	13	12	11	10	09	08	07	06	05	04	03	02			

CONTENTS

Introducing
Augustine

"Why do you mean so much to me?
Help me find the words to explain."
AUGUSTINE

Want to know God better? Augustine of Hippo did. Looking inside his heart he discovered an inward yearning for God that he was able to put on the written page. *"Our hearts are restless,"* he wrote, *"because you have made us for yourself and our hearts find no peace until they rest in you."*[1] For centuries those who have experienced spiritual passion to be filled with God have discovered in Augustine a friend, companion and guide.

Augustine was the bishop of a modest port city, Hippo Regis, in Africa for thirty-five years. He lived from A.D. 354 to 430, during the twilight years of the Roman Empire. Raised in the home of a devoted Christian mother, Monica, he lost what little faith he had acquired in his youth and lived a wild life as a graduate student. Initially interested in rhetorical law, he found that he excelled in learning and teaching philosophy. This thirst for truth led Augustine to embrace Manichaeanism—a cultlike mixture of Christian and Jewish ideas. Manichaeans saw Jesus as one of many saviors, a god-like being who did not have a real body and, therefore, could

---

[1]Augustine, *Confessions* 1.1, trans. R. S. Pine-Coffin (New York: Penguin, 1961).

not really suffer at his crucifixion. Manichaeanism billed itself as an advancement on the teaching of Christianity.

Meanwhile, Augustine was named to several prestigious positions as educator in the Roman Empire and became an esteemed teacher in the city of Rome itself. During his dozen years as a Manichaean, Augustine began to see the flaws in this "faith." The philosophy of Neoplatonism showed him different connections between mind and body and soul. The sermons of Ambrose, bishop of Milan, revealed Jesus as fully God and fully man—and as the redeemer of humans chained in "original sin." Looking again into the Christian faith, this time with the eyes of a philosopher, he began to discover answers that satisfied him. However, he resisted conversion—he was reticent to give up sexual pleasures. "God give me chastity and continence, but not just now" was the attitude of his heart. Then the persistent prayers and care of his mother, Monica, took root. Augustine found himself being drawn into the Christian faith, and one fateful day he stepped across the line and inside the faith.

It was a painful step. As was common in his culture among young men not yet suitably mature for marriage, Augustine had taken a mistress. He had been faithful to this mistress for fifteen years. They had a son named Adeodatus (gift of God) who died as a boy. At his conversion, Augustine left this relationship, in spite of the tears of his mistress, and took up the life of a monk. The Augustinian monastic order today still carries his name.

This guide is written to help you join those who have been spiritually challenged and enriched by Augustine's articulate passion for God. He published over ninety-three books and hundreds of sermons. We are going to sample from two of his best-known works, the *Confessions* and *The City of God.*

The *Confessions* is an exploration of a human heart—Augustine's heart. As one of the best-trained minds of his age, Augustine turns all his training and mind power inward. No one before him had attempted such an inward exploration. He has been described as a spelunker delving into the depths of the human soul. Although Augustine spends considerable time on sin in the *Confessions,* his purpose is not to air his dirty laundry; he wants to know God. We are going to look at three selections from the *Confessions*. The first study samples Augustine's passionate hunger for God, the second, his sense of sin, and the third, the account of his conversion. These three studies are intended to sample the three generally accepted meanings of what Augustine meant by confession: praise for God, confession of sin and profession of faith.

The City of God, a massive work that took some thirteen years to write and is encyclopedic in its scope, was written to answer charges raised by the pagan cultural elite against the Christian faith.[2] Using all his classical learning he not only exposes the foolish inconsistencies in the arguments of his opponents, he provides a new way to think about this world in light of the one to come. The City of Man and its citizens are on a downward slope toward destruction, but the City of God and its citizens are on an upward pilgrimage toward eternal fulfillment in the presence of God. In the three studies from *The City of God* we will see how Augustine rises to the defense of the faith, how he establishes a biblical framework for his perspective of life seen through the lens of the divine city and why Christians live in anticipation of heaven.

Augustine wrote while the classical world was dying, its brilliant culture collapsing into what we have come to call the Dark Ages. On the edge of the darkness Augustine was a primary source of light by which Christians were able to shine as the predominate influence. Like Augustine, we live in a time of change and moral confusion. Many are beginning to suspect that no matter how much we learn, work, produce and experience, there is something missing. They need to see in Christians a passionate hunger for God that speaks intelligently to their needs, concerns and confusions. A fresh look at Augustine can inspire us to both new depths of spiritual growth and a credible witness of the love of God that comes through faith in Jesus Christ.

---

[2]Augustine, *The City of God,* ed. Vernon J. Bourke, trans. Gerald G. Walsh et al. (New York: Doubleday, 1958).

How to Use a Christian Classics Bible Study
Christian Classics Bible studies are designed to introduce some of
the key writers, preachers and teachers who have shaped our
Christian thought over the centuries. Each guide has an introduction to the life and thought of a particular writer and six study sessions. The studies each have an introduction to the particular
themes and writings in that study and the following components.

READ
This is an excerpt from the original writings.

GROUP DISCUSSION OR PERSONAL REFLECTION
These questions are designed to help you explore the themes
of the reading.

INTO THE WORD
This includes a key Scripture to read and explore induc-
tively. The text picks up on the themes of the study session.

ALONG THE ROAD
These are ideas to carry you further and deeper into the
themes of the study. Some can be used in a group session; many are
for personal use and reflection.

The study notes at the end of the guide offer further helps and
background on the study questions.

May these writings and studies enrich your life in Christ.

I

THE QUESTIONS OF A HUNGRY MIND

Psalm 145:1-9; 1 Peter 5:5-6;
Romans 10:9-17

*T*he signs are everywhere: movie, TV and opinion polls indicate a rise in spiritual interest. However, there is no cause for Christians to relax. While it is clear that people are asking questions about the spiritual, it is not clear that those who ask questions will find them answered by the Christian faith.

Augustine was a great preacher who preached thousands of sermons, publishing over three hundred of them. Yet it is not his sermons that make the greatest impact on believers and unbelievers, it is his questions. In the swirl of the religious marketplace of the fifth century A.D., Augustine's surprising strategy was not merely to preach but to ask questions. He had questions for God. And he had questions about himself. But he didn't hide those questions, he published them!

By making his questions public Augustine invited others to join him in his spiritual pursuit. Now, with me, you are responding to his invitation. As we join millions of others who have taken up that invitation over the past fifteen hundred years, we may learn not only about God but also how to speak to those who are looking again for divine aid in the midst of this spiritually hungry world.

HUNGRY FOR GOD? ——————————————————

CONFESSIONS 1.1

Can any praise be worthy of the Lord's majesty? [Psalm 144:3]. *How magnificent his strength! How inscrutable his wisdom* [Psalm 145:3]. Man is one of your creatures, Lord, and his instinct is to praise you. He bears about him the mark of death, the sign of his own sin, to remind him that you *thwart the proud* [1 Peter 5:5]. But still, since he is a part of your creation, he wishes to praise you. The thought of you stirs him so deeply that he cannot be content unless he praises you, because you have made us for yourself and our hearts find no peace until they rest in you.

Grant me, Lord, to know and understand whether a man is first to pray to you for help or to praise you, and whether he must know you before he can call you to his aid. If he does not know you, how can he pray to you? For he may call for some other help, mistaking it for yours.

Or are men to pray to you and learn to know you through their prayers? *Only, how are they to call upon the Lord until they have learned to believe in him? And how are they to believe in him without a preacher to listen to?* [Romans 10:14].

Those who look for the Lord will cry out in praise of him [Psalm 22:26], because all who look for him shall find him, and when they find him they will praise him. I shall look for you, Lord, by praying to you and as I pray I shall believe in you, because we have had preachers to tell us about you. It is my faith that calls you, Lord, the faith which you gave me and made to live in me through the merits of your Son, who became man, and through the ministry of your preacher.

 GROUP DISCUSSION OR PERSONAL REFLECTION ——

1. As you read this opening section of the *Confessions,* what is your response?

Select a couple of phrases that stand out to you and explain why
you chose them.

2. Augustine begins his *Confessions* in paragraph one of section
one by quoting psalms which celebrate the Lord's greatness. How
does this way of "confession" differ from the way we generally think
about it?

3. Augustine is writing his confession in order to make it public.
What concerns would you have if you were asked to make a public
confession?

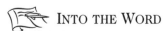 INTO THE WORD ————————————————————

4. *Read Psalm 145:1-9.* In the first paragraph Augustine quotes from the psalms and sets the tone for all that is to follow in *The Confessions*. What words would you use to describe the psalmist's view of God?

How does Augustine's writing reflect the content and tone of Psalm 145?

5. *Read 1 Peter 5:5-6.* Drawing from the Scriptures, Augustine's view of life is different from the arrogance that marked classical Roman culture of his time. How does Augustine's writing express Peter's call for humility?

Why is humility essential to being a healthy human?

6. Look at the second and third paragraphs of section one. Consider the questions Augustine asks, and summarize what you think he is struggling with.

7. *Read Romans 10:9-17.* After considering basic mysteries about approaching God through prayer, Augustine turns again to the Scriptures, quoting Romans 10:14. After reading the context of Romans 10:9-17 consider how this passage addresses the problem of knowing God.

8. What roles does faith play in knowing God, both in the Romans passage and in the final paragraph of section one?

9. Some have described Augustine's approach to God as intellectual, others have described it as passionate, still others as searching. From the reading in this session, how would you characterize it?

10. Augustine expresses spiritual hunger in a desire to praise God and understand prayer. How do you experience spiritual hunger?

11. As you finish this first glimpse of the *Confessions,* take a few moments to reflect: what can you confess that you like or appreciate about God?

 Along the Road ————————————————————

Augustine wrote out his prayerful confession. As we read it, we get a glimpse into his character and his understanding of the character of God. This week, take time daily to write out your prayerful confession to God. As you write, seek to use questions as Augustine did. At the end of the week look over what you have written so that you see what it reflects about your character and your understanding of the character of God.

II

CONFESSION IS GOOD FOR THE SOUL
Psalm 32

When my sons stepped over a line, I was quite willing to tell them they had done something wrong. But I don't remember ever telling them they had sinned. I guess I thought it would have sounded harsh and condemning. For many reasons, *sin* is a word that has dropped out of our vocabulary. In 1973 Karl Menninger, a renowned psychiatrist, published a book titled *Whatever Became of Sin?* Now more than ever, that is a good question, and one we should pay attention to.

As Augustine was writing his *Confessions,* sin was a hot topic in the church. Pelagius, a Celtic monk from the British Isles, was teaching that sin is not an intrinsic part of human nature in a fallen world. According to Pelagius it was possible for someone with enough willpower and determination to live a virtuous life that was pleasing to God.

In his later writings Augustine showed how Pelagius's teachings were destructive and in conflict both with Scripture and human experience. From his studies of the great Greek and Roman philosophers and from Scripture, he concluded that for all the discussion of the good life (and there was a great deal) in classical thought, there is a tragic flaw in human nature such that no one was capable of consistently living up to the simplest moral standards.

Confessions, however, is not an abstract theological rebuttal on the presence of sin in human nature. Here Augustine turned all his intellectual power inward on himself as exhibit A.

 ## THE HOUSE OF THE SOUL

CONFESSIONS 1.5

My soul is like a house, small for you to enter, but I pray you to enlarge it. It is in ruins, but I ask you to remake it. It contains much that you will not be pleased to see: this I know and do not hide. But who is to rid it of these things? There is no one but you to whom I can say: *if I have sinned unwittingly, do you absolve me. Keep me ever your own servant, far from pride* [Psalm 19:12, 13]. *I trust, and trusting I find words to utter* [Psalm 116:10]. Lord, you know that this is true. For have I not *made my transgressions known to you?* Did you not *remit the guilt of my sin* [Psalm 32:5]? I do not wrangle with you for judgment, for you are Truth itself, and I have no wish to delude myself, for fear that my malice should be self-betrayed. No, I do not wrangle with you, for, *if you, Lord, will keep record of our iniquities, Master, who has strength to bear it* [Psalm 130:3]?

CONFESSIONS 2.1

I must now carry my thought back to the abominable things I did in those days, the sins of the flesh which defiled my soul. I do this, my God, not because I love those sins, but so that I may love you. For love of your love I shall retrace my wicked ways. The memory is bitter, but it will help me to savour your sweetness, the sweetness that does not deceive but brings real joy and never fails. For love of your love I shall retrieve myself from the havoc of disruption which

tore me to pieces when I turned away from you, whom alone I
should have sought, and lost myself instead on many a different
quest. For as I grew to manhood I was inflamed with desire for a
surfeit of hell's pleasures. Foolhardy as I was, I ran wild with lust
that was manifold and rank. In your eyes my beauty vanished and I
was foul to the core, yet I was pleased with my own condition and
anxious to be pleasing in the eyes of men.

GROUP DISCUSSION OR PERSONAL REFLECTION

1. From these two paragraphs of the *Confessions,* why do you
think Augustine felt that it was important to take a careful look at
his own sin?

2. Guilt has led many into a life of spiritual avoidance. Why
doesn't Augustine feel a need to suppress his sense of guilt and sinfulness and run from God?

3. *Repression* is a term used to describe attempts to avoid facing
painful experiences. What benefit does Augustine expect from
exposing his sin rather than repressing it?

4. How would you describe the emotional elements of Augustine's relationship to God?

How would you describe the emotional elements of your relationship with God?

5. Augustine describes his soul as a small house in need of renovation. Using his image of the soul as a house, how would you describe the size and condition of your soul?

 INTO THE WORD————————————————

6. *Read Psalm 32.* According to David, the author of this psalm, confession is indeed good for the soul. What is wrong with keeping your sins to yourself (vv. 3-4)?

7. For a period of time, David chose silence rather than confession. What is it about sin that makes us want to keep it a secret?

8. How are the horse and mule (v. 9) apt images of those who avoid confession?

9. Look back at verses 1-2. David describes those who are forgiven as blessed. What has been your personal experience of being forgiven?

10. How is it possible to be a sinner (v. 1) yet "upright in heart" (v. 11)?

11. Protection and instruction are given to those who are faithful (vv. 6-8). From your reflection on this psalm, what do these gifts from God have to do with confession?

12. Read over the selection of the *Confessions* one more time. What influences from Psalm 32 can you see in Augustine's writing?

 ALONG THE ROAD ───────────────────────

An exploration of your past behavior and the dynamics of sin would require keeping a journal like Augustine did. Choose a limited period in your life in which you might explore the dynamics of sin. Using Augustine as your model spend some time each day journaling through attitudes and actions that need to be confessed in the light of God's presence.

III

CONTINUING CONVERSION
Acts 9:1-22

*C*hristians differ in their views of how conversion takes place. I grew up in a church that disapproved of "those kind of Christians who talked about conversions and being *born again*." I left that church in my adolescent years because I didn't find the spiritual resources I needed to cope with several family tragedies. Several years later I was converted through the influence of a church that believed that all members of the church should be able to name the exact time and place in which they made a decision for Jesus. I am now a pastor in a church that emphasizes the fruit of conversion—the issue is not when or how you were converted, but the necessity of having a present relationship with God through Jesus Christ that expresses itself in godly behavior.

How should we think about conversion? Augustine can help us. The selection which follows is one of the most famous conversion accounts in all of Christian history. Augustine records his movement from the doubts, fears and hesitations of the past. As one door closes behind him, another one opens to God, and he finds a conviction that frees him to believe and follow Christ into daily practice of a godly life.

HEARING THE VOICE OF GOD ————————————

CONFESSIONS 8.12

Whether it was the voice of a boy or a girl I cannot say, but again and again it repeated the refrain "Take it and read, take it and read." At this I looked up, thinking hard whether there was any kind of game in which children used to chant words like these, but I could not remember ever hearing them before. I stemmed my flood of tears and stood up, telling myself that this could only be a divine command to open my book of Scripture and read the first passage on which my eyes should fall. For I had heard the story of Antony, and I remembered how he had happened to go to a church while the Gospel was being read and had taken it as a counsel addressed to himself when he heard the words *Go home and sell all that belongs to you. Give it to the poor, and so the treasure you have shall be in heaven; then come back and follow me* [Matthew 19:21]. By this divine pronouncement he had at once been converted to you.

So I hurried back to the place where Alypius was sitting, for when I stood up to move away I had put down the book containing Paul's Epistles. I seized it and opened it, and in silence I read the first passage on which my eyes fell: *Not in revelling and drunkenness, not in lust and wantonness, not in quarrels and rivalries. Rather, arm yourselves with the Lord Jesus Christ; spend no more thought on nature and nature's appetites* [Romans 13:13, 14]. I had no wish to read more and no need to do so. For in an instant, as I came to the end of the sentence, it was as though the light of confidence flooded my heart and all the darkness of doubt was dispelled. . . .

Then we went in and told my mother, who was overjoyed. And when we went on to describe how it had all happened, she was jubilant with triumph and glorified you, *who are powerful enough, and more than powerful enough, to carry out your purpose beyond all our hopes and dreams* [Ephesians 3:20]. For she saw that you had granted her far more than she used to ask in her tearful prayers and plaintive lamentations. You converted me to yourself, so that I no longer desired a wife or placed any hope in this world but stood firmly upon the rule of faith, where you had shown me to her in a dream so many years before. And you *turned her sadness into rejoicing* [Psalm 30:11], into joy far fuller than her dearest wish.

 GROUP DISCUSSION OR PERSONAL REFLECTION ——

1. Augustine overhears a child's voice and senses that God is speaking to him. When and in what ways have you sensed God speaking to you through a person or an experience?

2. As Augustine ponders what to do about the voice he hears, he recalls the conversion account of Antony, reputed to be the first great contemplative of the church. What role do the Scriptures occupy in the conversion of both Antony and Augustine?

What do the two Scriptures that influenced Antony and Augustine have in common?

3. How does Augustine's conversion bring together both faith and continuing obedience?

4. Although this was a significant turning point in Augustine's life, his journey had taken years of reflection and continual prayers by Augustine's devoted mother—as well as the witness of many other significant Christian figures of his era. Who has been influential in the development of your Christian commitment?

 INTO THE WORD————————————————————

5. *Read Acts 9:1-22.* This is the account of Paul's conversion, perhaps the most famous conversion recorded in Scripture. How would you describe the interaction between Saul and Jesus (vv. 4-5)?

6. How does Paul's conversion compare to Augustine's?

7. This is a dramatic change for Paul. What questions, fears and feelings might he have faced during his three days of blindness (v. 9)?

8. Instead of speaking directly to Paul after those dark three days, the Lord sends Ananias (vv. 10-17). How would this divinely arranged meeting have been important to both Paul and Ananias?

9. The word *conversion* means change. As you read through the passage, what changes take place in Paul's life?

10. You may have grown up in a Christian home and lived a consistent life, or you may have had a dramatic change and some specific turning point. Regardless of how your conversion happened, what changes mark your life as a follower of Jesus Christ?

11. Saul's conversion meant a call to Christ's gospel, hardship and suffering, along with a mutually dependent relationship with Christ's people (vv. 10-17). Which of those elements are present in your Christian experience?

12. Ananias was sent to welcome Saul into the faith and bring a further word from the Lord. What role have you, or might you have, in welcoming those who are converted into the community of Jesus' followers?

 ALONG THE ROAD ————————————————————

❷ Both Ananias and Monica were significant contributors to the growth of the church through their care and hospitality to Paul and Augustine. Who has been a contributor to your growth?

Each day this week write a brief note of appreciation to those who have been helpful to you along the way in your Christian pilgrimage.

❷ Ask God if there are one or two individuals that he would like you to prayerfully support, either in coming to conversion or perhaps being encouraged to new levels of Christian growth. After you have discerned who the Lord is calling you to, begin to pray for them on a regular basis.

IV

Defending
the Faith

1 Peter 2:9-17

After my conversion I was eager to share my faith with my friends and family—well, I was mostly eager. I was also more than a little defensive. I was sure that some people would think I had pitched my brain out the door and become a religious fanatic.

In order to share my faith and cope with feelings of defensiveness I began to pay more attention to my studies in college. I even enrolled in seminary, not to become a minister but to understand what Christianity was all about so that I could better explain it to others.

In *The City of God* Augustine moves from confessing his faith to defending it as he seeks to provide answers to arguments raised against Christianity. Just like many of the leading thinkers of the modern world, the leading thinkers and trendsetters of classical Roman culture had widespread objections to Christianity. Since the "sack of Rome" in 410 by the Vandals, it was alleged that the old pagan gods were no longer protecting Rome, and that the Christian God had failed to come through for the city in its time of need. Augustine took up the challenge of exposing such charges as foolish and inconsistent.

From Augustine we learn ways to respond to the widespread objections to Christianity that we face in our day. Instructed by him, we can gain new confidence and at the same time remove obstacles that hinder objectors from seriously considering the Christian faith.

 ## BLAME THE CHRISTIANS? ——————————————

THE CITY OF GOD 1.36

I still have something to say against those who hold our religion responsible for the disaster to the Roman state, because it has forbidden them to sacrifice to their gods. Here, I must remind you of all the grave calamities which have occurred (or as many as will suffice for my purpose), and which the city itself, or the provinces subject to its rule, had to endure long before their sacrifices were banned. . . .

Then, I must show on account of what virtues and for what reason the true God, in whose power are all kingdoms, vouchsafed His help to spread the empire, while those fictions they call god gave no help at all, but, on the contrary, worked untold harm by their deceptions and frauds.

THE CITY OF GOD 2.3

Bear in mind that in recounting these things, I am still dealing with those ignorant dupes who gave birth and popular currency to the saying: "If there is a drought, blame the Christians." . . . In order to arouse popular hatred against us, they pretend ignorance and strive to instill into people's minds the common notion that the misfortunes which afflict the human race are due to the expansion of Christianity and the eclipse of the pagan gods by the bright glory of its reputation and renown.

Let them, therefore, recall with me the calamities which so often and in so many ways set back the prosperity of Rome, and remember, too, that all this happened long before Christ came in the flesh, long before His Name shone before men with that glory which they vainly begrudge Him. In the face of those disasters, let them defend their gods if they can, remembering that they were worshiped precisely to prevent the evils recorded. Yet, if any of the evils befall them now, we Christians must bear the blame. Why then, did the gods permit the misfortunes I shall mention to fall on their devotees before the promulgation of Christ's teaching provoked their wrath and proscribed their sacrifices?

 GROUP DISCUSSION OR PERSONAL REFLECTION ——

1. Augustine is going to address charges directed against Christians for the calamities of the Roman Empire. What objections do you hear being raised against the Christian faith in our time?

2. What inconsistencies does Augustine point out in the arguments of Christianity's detractors?

3. Pagans resented that the spreading influence of Christianity stopped them from offering sacrifices to their gods. What do con-

temporary pagans resent about the influence of Christianity?

 INTO THE WORD———————————————————————

4. *Read 1 Peter 2:9-17.* From the guidance Peter gives, what charges do you think were being made against Christians in the first century?

5. Peter emphasizes the privileged identity of Christians (vv. 9-10). What is special about Christians?

How do you feel "special" and "privileged" as a Christian?

6. The privileged identity of Christians means that we are aliens and strangers in the world (v. 11). Are there ways in which you feel like an alien and stranger to those around you who don't share the Christian faith?

7. Peter's prescription for dealing with charges and objections to the Christian faith begins with personal moral conduct (v. 11). How does immoral behavior on the part of Christians provide ammunition for Christian detractors?

8. In contrast to the negative impact of ungodly immoral behavior, how is godly moral behavior a commendation for the Christian faith?

9. Peter's second prescription for dealing with charges and objections to the Christian faith could be described as "Be a good citizen" (vv. 13-17). According to Peter, what are the essentials of good citizenship?

How does unruly public behavior lead people to negative assumptions about Christianity?

10. You are being watched! How does the knowledge that others are evaluating Christianity in light of your behavior affect you?

11. Peter expects the quality of Christian conduct to silence ignorant accusations (v. 15) and bring glory to God (v. 12). What good have Christians contributed to the world that can be pointed out to accusers and objectors?

What can you personally do to counter objections to Christianity?

 ALONG THE ROAD ———————————————————

❧ Internal motivations have eternal consequences not only for believers but for those who don't yet know Christ. Do a "heart check" this week and determine to be a witness by your attitudes and attractions toward others.

❧ One of Peter's requirements for demonstrating the gospel is to abstain from sinful desires which war against your soul. In a culture where all desires are considered normal, this is a radical change. This week carefully ponder the motivations and desires; intentionally say "no" to those which would lead to ungodly behavior. At the end of the week add up the number of times you restrained yourself. Also pay attention to how you respond to such restraints, and make this a matter of prayerful conversation with God.

❧ Consider your attitude toward those who have authority over you. In a time in which "attitude" is considered by many to be essential, prayerful respect requires a radical change. At the end of the week consider how your inward and outward behavior compares with your normal way of living.

V

THE TWO CITIES

Hebrews 11:8-16

*M*y family, along with a group of college students, spent most of one summer on a short-term mission trip to the small Central American country of Belize. On the Fourth of July the American consulate invited all Americans in Belize City to a holiday celebration. Throughout the afternoon we gathered at the consulate, eating hot dogs, drinking Coke and Pepsi, and chatting with other Americans. I was surprised at the depth of kinship and patriotic feelings I experienced with people I had never met before. While we may have been from opposite ends of the country, we had much in common. Together we were aliens and strangers in a foreign land, and this experience made us especially proud to be Americans.

Romans, too, had a strong sense of patriotism. Rome itself was a city that gleamed in the sun as all its major public buildings were constructed of marble. Roman engineers built roads that spread across Europe and aqueducts that brought running water into public baths and private homes. Its leading citizens were wealthy beyond compare. Roman armies were the most powerful in the world. With nearly one thousand years of history and an empire that controlled the entire civilized world, they had good reason for pride. No wonder Romans thought of Rome as the Eternal City.

In answer to the charges raised by skeptical cultural leaders, Augustine continued to assert that the problems which Roman culture now faced were not the fault of Christians. Augustine effectively turned the tables. He agreed that there is an eternal city which is the standard of all others, but that eternal city is neither Rome nor any earthly city. Instead the standard is a heavenly one: the city of God.

The root problem was that the Roman elite were not living in the true eternal city but a humanly constructed one—a city bound to chaos and disorder because it lived in conflict with its true God and Creator.

GOD'S HOME

THE CITY OF GOD 11.1

The expression, "City of God," which I have been using is justified by that Scripture. . . . We read: "Glorious things are said of thee, O city of God" [Psalm 86:3]; and in another psalm: "Great is the Lord, and exceedingly to be praised in the city of our God, in His holy mountain, increasing the joy of the whole earth"; and a little later in the same psalm: "As we have heard, so we have seen, in the city of the Lord of hosts, in the city of our God: God hath founded it for ever" [Psalm 47:1, 2, 9]; and in another text: "The stream of the river maketh the city of God joyful: the most High hast sanctified his own tabernacle. God is in the midst thereof, it shall not be moved" [Psalm 45:5, 6].

Through these and similar passages too numerous to quote, we learn of the existence of a City of God whose Founder has inspired us with a love and a longing to become its citizens. The inhabitants of the earthly city who prefer their own gods to the Founder of the holy City do not realize that He is the God of gods.

THE CITY OF GOD 14.1

This is the reason why, for all the difference of the many and very great nations throughout the world in religion and morals, language, weapons, and dress, there exist no more than the two kinds of society, which, according to the Scriptures, we have rightly called the two cities. One city is that of men who live according to the flesh. The other is of men who live according to the spirit. Each of them chooses its own kind of peace and, when they attain what they desire, each lives in the peace of its own choosing.

 GROUP DISCUSSION OR PERSONAL REFLECTION———

1. Augustine says that all humanity can be divided into the human city and the divine city. What positive associations come to mind when you think of the word *city?*

What negative associations?

2. From the Scriptures Augustine cites (and others you can think of), what do you see as the difference between the city of God and the city of humanity?

3. In contrasting the city of God with the city of humanity, what do you think he means by "each lives by the peace of its own choosing"?

4. How might Augustine's perspective of the city of God open up fresh and rich spiritual insights into your experience of the Christian faith?

 INTO THE WORD ─────────────────────────

5. *Read Hebrews 11:8-16.* The author of Hebrews captures the heart of the New Testament teaching on the heavenly city in these verses. As you read through the passage, consider how you would describe the impact and influence of this vision of the heavenly city.

6. How are both faith and hope active in Abraham as he sets out for the Promised Land (v. 9)?

7. Because Abraham and Sarah were beyond childbearing years, they had no earthly hope of having a child (v. 10). What kept them hoping?

8. Living in tents reminded Abraham and his family that there was something more certain and solid coming in the future. What reminds you that there is something more certain and solid coming in God's promised eternal future?

9. Just as Peter described Christians as aliens and strangers, the writer of Hebrews portrays Abraham's family as aliens and strangers (v. 13). How is it that Abraham's family could be characterized as aliens when they were living in the land that God promised to them?

10. What does it mean to welcome God's promised land from a distance (v. 13)?

11. How is it that the promise of eternal life not only gives us hope for the future but also strengthens us in the present?

12. Because heaven is beyond our experience and therefore beyond our imagination, how might it be helpful to think of heaven as an eternal city?

13. How might citizenship in the heavenly city help make you a better citizen of the earthly "city" where you live now?

ALONG THE ROAD ————————————————

Reflect on the following scriptural truths in your devotional time this next week. Ask God to use them to provide new perspectives on living the Christian life.

Day 1: Through faith in Jesus Christ I am a citizen of the heavenly city and choose to live today in hopeful anticipation of what awaits me in eternity.

Day 2: Through faith in Jesus Christ I am a citizen of the heavenly city and choose to live today persevering through the challenges and struggles I encounter because I know they are only temporary.

Day 3: Through faith in Jesus Christ I am a citizen of the heavenly city and choose to live today with a wise detachment because I know that all I have and all I experience are incomplete.

Day 4: Through faith in Jesus Christ I am a citizen of the heavenly city and choose to live today as an active citizen of my earthly community because I know that it points me toward all that is yet to come.

Day 5: Through faith in Jesus Christ I am a citizen of the heavenly city and choose to live today in faith because I know that I can trust God to bring me safely to my eternal home.

VI

THE CITY OF GOD
Revelation 21:1-8

*I*n my adolescence I was an avid reader of science fiction, at one point devouring at least one book a week. The "future" in those books was often portrayed as a place in which amazing machines produced a society of contented people who had ample leisure to enjoy the fruits of humanly constructed technological utopia.

I'm not such a fan anymore. That bright and shining future has been severely tarnished, to the point of extinction. Whether a place of genetic manipulation and slavery as first portrayed by Aldous Huxley in *Brave New World,* or dark and dreary corruption of sprawling cities populated by humans and androids in the classic sci-fi movie *Blade Runner,* those who think about the future see it as anything but a humanly created technological utopia where all evils are eradicated and human desires fulfilled. Now the future is depicted as a scary place in which the unleashed forces of biology, electronics and physics create unforeseen terrors with no known solutions.

Augustine would not be surprised that some of our greatest imaginative thinkers see the future darkly. He wrote the voluminous *City of God* to confront the foolish and unfounded hopefulness of the pagan leaders of his day. Yes, he says, it is true that the city of humanity leads downward into death and darkness. But that is not all! There is more to life than just the city of humanity. *The City of God* beckons us to a future that is indeed bright and shining and full of hope.

 THE SOURCE OF HOPE ————————————————

THE CITY OF GOD 22.1

As I mentioned in the preceding Book, the present one is to be the last of the whole work, and is to deal with the eternal blessedness of the City of God. The word "eternal" as here used means more than any period, however long, of centuries upon centuries which, ultimately, must have an end. It means "everlasting" in the sense of the text which runs: "Of His kingdom there shall be no end" [Luke 1:33]. It does not mean the kind of apparent perpetuity produced by successive generations which come and go by births and deaths. Such a perpetuity is merely perennial like the color of an evergreen that seems to continue forever because the new leaves, sprouting while the old ones wither and fall, maintain an unchanging density of foliage. On the contrary, in the eternal City of God, each and all of the citizens are personally immortal with an immortality which the holy angels never lost and which even human beings can come to share.

THE CITY OF GOD 22.30

The conclusion is that, in the everlasting City, there will remain in each and all of us an inalienable freedom of the will, emancipating us from every evil and filling us with every good, rejoicing in the inexhaustible beatitude of everlasting happiness, unclouded by the memory of any sin or of sanction suffered, yet with no forgetfulness of our redemptions nor any loss of gratitude for our Redeemer.

Heaven, too, will be the fulfillment of that Sabbath rest foretold in the command: "Be still and see that I am God" [Psalm 45:11]. This, indeed, will be the ultimate Sabbath that has no evening and which the Lord foreshadowed in the account of His creation [Genesis 2:2, 3]. . . . And we ourselves will be a "seventh day" when we shall be filled with His blessing and remade by His sanctification. In the stillness of that rest we shall see that he is the God whose divinity we ambitioned for ourselves when we listened to the seducer's words, "You shall be as Gods" [Genesis 3:5], and so fell away from Him, the true God who would have given us a dignity by participation that could never be gained by desertion.

 GROUP DISCUSSION OR PERSONAL REFLECTION——

1. Augustine makes clear that there is a difference in quality of life in the eternal city from that which we now experience. What is the difference and why is it important?

2. How is the freedom of the city of God different from the freedom that most are looking for today?

3. What unity does Augustine see between the ultimate end of the human race and its first beginnings?

 INTO THE WORD ────────────────────

4. *Read Revelation 21:1-8.* Just as Rome was the center of the empire, the new Jerusalem is the center of a renewed creation. What is the new city in the new creation like?

5. There is an emphasis on newness of all creation. What would it be like if God allowed you to stay the same and renewed everything around you?

What would it be like if God renewed you but kept everything around you the same?

6. It might seem strange that this passage describes an impending marriage of God to the new city. What elements and dynamics of marriage can you discover in this passage?

7. In verse 3 the dwelling of God is said to be among humanity. How is this different than it had been?

8. One of the benefits of the continuing presence of God in the new creation is that death and all sources of pain will be removed. How does pain affect and influence your life?

What do you think it would be like to be free of pain?

9. How is the vision of the new Jerusalem different from the communist vision of a perfect society?

How does the vision of the new Jerusalem differ from the American dream?

10. God, seated on the throne, describes himself as the *Alpha* and the *Omega,* the first and last letters of the Greek alphabet. How is God's presence in the first creation similar to his presence in the new creation?

How is it different?

11. As Augustine attempted to show, there is a distinction in the human experience between the city of God and the city of humanity. What distinguishes those who are inside the city from those who aren't?

12. The city of God brings a fundamental challenge to all of life. Although citizenship in the city of God is by grace, it is a gift given to those who overcome. How would you explain this paradox?

How does this promise of eternal citizenship in God's city challenge you?

 ALONG THE ROAD ————————————————

Augustine has been described as a spelunker who delved into the depths of the human heart. Using the themes of this guide as rungs on a ladder, each day take one step deeper into your heart, seeking to draw closer to God. Like Augustine who wrote of his inward journey, you will find it helpful to record your reflections in a journal. Augustine wrote frequently of his love for God; as you write, give yourself freedom to put in writing your own love of God.

Day 1: Explore your heart for signs of hunger to worship God. Ponder what it feels like to love God and desire him.

Day 2. Explore your sense of sin. How does sin show itself in your thoughts, attitudes and actions? by what you do and by what you leave undone? in your relationships with family and friends?

Day 3. Consider afresh your conversion. What was it that induced you to stop avoiding God and to give yourself to him? How do the ripples of your surrender to God continue to work their way through the depths of your being?

Day 4. Consider objections and reservations to the gospel. Which seem most credible to you? How do God's Spirit and God's Word work in your heart to address your concerns?

Day 5. Explore your desire for life in this world and your anticipation for heaven. How much is the hunger for God accompanied by a hunger for heaven? There is a this-worldly focus in our culture that redirects our thinking away from heaven. As you journal, ask God to uncover that hunger for heaven that his Spirit has placed in your heart.

Day 6. Continue to explore your hunger for heaven. Can you find a "heavenly homesickness" inside? What does it feel like to long for heaven? In what ways does a longing for heaven affect the way you think and act?

How to Lead a Christian Classics Bible Study

If you are leading a small group discussion using this series, we have good news for you: you do not need to be an expert on Christian history. We have provided the information you need about the historical background in the introduction to each study. Reading more of the original work of these writers will be helpful but is not necessary. We have set each reading in context within the introductions to each study. Further background and helps are found in the study notes to each session as well. And a bibliography is provided at the end of each guide.

In leading the Bible study portion of each study you will be helped by a resource like *Leading Bible Discussions* in our LifeGuide® Bible Study series as well as books dealing with small group dynamics like *The Big Book on Small Groups*. But, once again, you do not need to be an expert on the Bible. The Bible studies are designed to follow the flow of the passage from observation to interpretation to application. You may feel that the studies lead themselves! The study notes at the back will help you through the tough spots.

What Is Your Job as a Leader?

☐ To pray that God will be at work in your heart and mind as well as in the hearts and minds of the group members.

☐ To thoroughly read all of the studies, Scripture texts and all of the helps in this guide before the study.

☐ To help people to feel comfortable as they arrive and to encourage everyone to participate in the discussion.

☐ To encourage group members to apply what they are learning in the study session and by using the "Along the Road" sections between sessions.

Study Notes

Study One. The Questions of a Hungry Mind. Psalm 145:1-9; 1 Peter 5:5-6; Romans 10:9-17.

Purpose: To explore the nature of spiritual hunger and intimacy with God.

Question 1. This first question intends to help your group read intentionally. You might want to give yourself and the group time to read over the material a few times. Be sure to encourage lots of contributions by asking several times, "What else impressed you?"

This is also an opportunity to point out the phrase at the end of the first paragraph "you made us for yourself and our hearts find no peace until they rest in you." This is one of the most famous in all of Christian literature. I personally like the first part of this phrase: "The thought of you stirs him so deeply that he cannot be content unless he praises you." These words deeply resonate with me as I find that there are times, usually during quiet moments when I am sitting in my backyard, that I yearn to praise God and occasionally discover that words can't even express the hunger I feel to show praise and thanksgiving.

Question 2. Augustine does not mean for his confession to be merely an exposure of his sinfulness. He has a broader view of confession in mind. Our use of the word *testimony* actually captures the essence of his confession. As he confesses his spiritual journey, including his sin, he is going to testify to the greatness of God.

Question 3. Certainly courage and humility are qualities for a public confession. But also a great deal of discretion. Knowing what to say and not to say are essential. Exposure of sin in public testimonies has in the past been an expression of pride and even arrogance as confessors used a public platform to draw attention to themselves. Augustine is very clear that he wants his confession to point us to the greatness of God.

Question 4. This is an opportunity to grow in the act of worship. Enjoy what the psalmist celebrates about God. Seek to develop the attitude of appreciation for who God is that lead from the lines of this psalm. Created by God, marked by sin, subject to death, human beings still have an innate need to worship their Creator. This is exactly what Augustine is doing in this first paragraph: worshiping God.

Question 5. Implicit in Augustine's view of human nature is a need to confess because there is much that is not right about us. Humility is therefore the only proper response to God.

Western culture has encouraged a posture of arrogance rather than humility. For example, humans are not viewed as sinful, fallen or abnormal: we are merely evolving. Death is not a work of God to thwart the proud but merely a part of the natural order. Morality means doing what we feel because whatever desires and feelings we have are natural.

Question 6. Augustine is struggling with how anyone comes to know God. He approaches the problem of the knowledge of God through prayer and questions rather than mere intellectual speculation and rational deduction.

Question 7. This passage gives the Christian answer to the problem of the knowledge of God: the gospel of Jesus Christ and those messengers sent to make him known.

Question 9. The purpose of this question is to stimulate reflection on the nature of Augustine's approach. Certainly Augustine is intellectual, passionate and searching. If I were asked to pick one idea that described his approach, I would choose the words *vulnerability* and *humility*. At the time he was writing, Augustine was already acknowledged as a great teacher of the church—yet he was willing to record his questions for God. And, as we shall see, he was willing to expose his sin, both past and present, in this act of inviting us to join in his pursuit of knowing God.

Question 10. Joyce Huggett once observed that words for "longing," "seeking" and "yearning" repeatedly surface in the writings of great spiritual teachers of the church. In my own studies of past spiritual masters I have discovered the word *sweet*. From Augustine in the fifth century, Bernard in the thirteenth or Jonathan Edwards in the eighteenth the word *sweet* frequently appears to describe that inner desire for God. Edwards writes, "Spiritual good is of a satisfying nature and the more man experiences this satisfying sweetness, the more earnestly he hungers and thirsts for it."

Study Two. Confession Is Good for the Soul. Psalm 32.
Purpose: To embrace the benefits of confessing our sins to God.
Question 1. Augustine developed the classic orthodox view of original sin: that all humans share in Adam and Eve's sin, and since their Fall into sin all humans are corporately infected. Pelagius's position makes it possible for humans to continue in self-deceit and in spiritual alienation from God. The result is that sin is never addressed, and intimacy with God is not possible. In other passages of the *Confessions,* Augustine appeals to Scriptures such as Psalm 51:5 and Romans 3:10, 23 in order to show the pervasive nature of sin.
Question 2. Augustine is convinced from the Scriptures that although God is the one we offend most with our sin, God is also the only one who has the ability to forgive it. Although God could justly destroy us because of our sin, he prefers to forgive us.
Question 3. Augustine desires intimacy with God. By confessing his sin he expects to be able to grow into new levels of being filled with God.
Question 4. Augustine twice refers to his motivation being "the love of the love of God." Passion, longing and affection are expressed throughout the *Confessions.* It is important for our spiritual health that we take the time and effort to cultivate an intimacy with God that includes our emotions. While some of us have been told that our relationship with God is based on fact not feeling, it is also true that healthy love has a very strong emotional element. In marriage, every couple goes through periods when the emotional element cools. Yet when there are extended periods of time in which emotion is absent, it means something is amiss. In a similar way, when there are extended periods of time in which emotion is absent toward God, something indeed is amiss.
Question 5. The image of the soul as a dwelling has been used profitably by other spiritual writers throughout church history. In the sixteenth century Teresa of Ávila spoke more grandly than Augustine of the soul as an "interior castle." In the twentieth century Robert Boyd Munger wrote a widely distributed booklet, *My Heart—Christ's Home.*

Question 6. David mentions two problems with keeping silent about sin. First, there are the physical and emotional effects of guilt that haunt him. Second, he understands the symptoms of sin not merely coming from his own sense of guilt but also from God whose hand of judgment was on him. The twelve-step recovery programs that help people address addictions include confession of past sins as an essential step in breaking the hold of addictions.

Question 7. As you and the members of your group answer this question, don't just accept simple answers like "pride," "shame" and the like. Encourage people to look into their own experiences of sin and ponder what made them actually avoid confessing it.

Question 8. Confession is a way of acknowledging that we are giving up living by our own agenda rather than God's. One of the primary reasons we do not have a sense of the will or the presence of God is because we are avoiding it. If we "hear him we won't have an excuse for continuing to go our own way rather than his." If we are to enjoy the presence of God, we must give up our stubborn determination to follow our own self-generated agenda.

Question 9. Encourage members of your group to think back to a specific situation in which they experienced forgiveness.

Question 10. Scripture acknowledges only two classes of people, "forgiven sinners" and "unforgiven sinners." In Scripture the righteous are not those who are morally perfect but those who have faith in God and are forgiven. The righteous are not those who are morally perfect—á la Pelagius—but those whose faith gives them the courage to seek God's grace.

Question 11. This question is really the flip side of question 8 (on the stubbornness of the horse and mule). While many with a superficial relationship with God may ask for his direction, only those who trust God to the depth of confessing their sin to him are willing to receive his direction and discipline.

Question 12. Augustine has learned from this psalm and other Scriptures that he needs to bring the depth of need into the light of God's presence. Instead of hiding his sin from the Lord, Augustine, like David, learns to bring his sin to the Lord (v. 5). As he begins an internal quest to expose the depth of his sin, he knows that by acknowledging his sinful past he puts himself in a place to be cleansed and guided.

Study Three. Continuing Conversion. Acts 9:1-22.

Purpose: To discover how following Christ means a life of continual change into deeper levels of obedience.

Question 1. This question highlights that the Christian faith is not merely about affirming a set of beliefs. It is also about a personal encounter with God, who is in constant communion with his people.

Question 2. Although God is free to speak to us in any way that he pleases, at the time of the Reformation the formulation "Word and Spirit" was developed. This formulation was intended to capture the dynamic of how God communicates in the present through what had been written in the past. Both Antony and Augustine sense the Word being applied to them as the Spirit quickens the Word to their hearts. Both Scriptures require an active expression of faith. Antony felt called to sell all he had, and Augustine felt called to a lifestyle that turned away from his promiscuous past.

Question 3. This question develops the preceding one. If it feels redundant, feel free to skip over it. It is intended to highlight Augustine's call to chastity and a life of heavenly anticipation. In a culture that is so this-world oriented, even Christians tend to think about the benefits of faith in Christ on this side of heaven. It is good for us to be reminded that much of what we are called to live is experienced on the other side of death.

Question 4. This question allows for a reference to Augustine's mother, Monica, who was a significant influence in his conversion. Throughout the *Confessions* he makes reference to her influence in his life. This question also provides an opportunity to put conversion in a broader context than merely a decision at a single point in time. It is possible to see the entire work of the *Confessions* as a record of continuing conversion as Augustine grew deeper into new life in Jesus Christ.

Question 5. The interaction is brief and to the point. Unlike Augustine, who resisted and hesitated for several years, once Paul saw the truth there was no hesitation. Jesus knew what Paul needed to hear. Paul, being a man of high intelligence and action, immediately got the point.

Question 6. Both do indeed have dramatic turning points. Both are "spoken to." Both share their conversion with others who affirm it. It is also worth noting that Augustine hears the word of the Lord through the words that Paul has written, as recorded in his letter to the Romans.

Question 7. Paul's reflection on the role of the law as bringing death, and as insufficient to change the heart, indicates that he was probably aware that Jewish religious practices were deficient even prior to his conversion. Just as we discover new insights about God throughout our lives, we also discover new ways that we are shaped by sin and live blindly by its insidious influences.

Question 9. Prior to his conversion Paul didn't believe in Jesus, afterward he did. Prior to his conversion Paul was a persecutor of the church, afterward he was a member of it. Prior to his conversion Paul preached against Christ, afterward he preached for Christ. Continuing change should mark the life of every believer, as there are always deeper levels of faith and obedience to which the Lord calls us.

Question 11. In some Christian circles there is a belief that once we accept Christ our troubles are over. Neither the recorded experience of the early church nor its teachings support such a way of thinking. Jesus tells Paul he must expect to suffer for Jesus' name. All of the apostles endured great hardships and most died violent deaths. While those in your study may not be experiencing persecution for their faith, the difficulties of being a consistent and faithful believer are present for every Christian in every age.

Question 12. Often we think of mission and evangelism as telling others about Jesus and inviting them to faith. We need to discover the role of hospitality in mission. There are many whom Jesus has called that need to be invited into the church and affirmed in the faith.

Study Four. Defending the Faith. 1 Peter 2:9-17.

Purpose: To discover how Christians can respond to objections to the gospel.

Background note. You are about to venture into the realm of apologetics. Apologetics in Christian theology does not mean making excuses for what you believe. It means answering objections raised by critics. The early church developed a number of key apologists who were able to aptly answer pagan objections. Of all the apologists of the early church Augustine was the most prolific and effective.

A key verse used as the foundational starting point of apologetics comes from 1 Peter 3:15-16, in which Peter writes, "Always be prepared to give an answer to everyone who asks you to give the reason for the hope that you have. But do this with gentleness and respect, keeping a clear conscience, so that those who speak maliciously against your good behavior in Christ may be ashamed of their slander."

Question 1. After my conversion I majored in apologetics (especially Francis Schaeffer's work), learning how to expose the philosophical inconsistencies of objectors in order to show that Christianity was rational and true. In recent years it seems to me that few object to Christianity as being unscientific and irrational. Instead, objections center on Christianity as intolerant of other faiths and approaches to morality.

Question 3. Contemporary pagans have a variety of resentments about the influence of Christianity—some justifiable, others not. Consider several that come to mind, along with ways you can address those objections. Quality of life and vitality of faith seem to me to be two essentials for countering objections and reservations to the Christian faith. There is a spiritual attractiveness to those who have a living faith and who show their faith by their attitudes and actions.

Question 4. It appears that Christians were accused of being rebels who refused to submit to the governmental authorities. Since Christians said, "Jesus is Lord," and refused to say, "Caesar is Lord," there was good reason for this accusation. Peter seeks to guide Christians in a life of discernment. While we are not to acknowledge any other Lord than Jesus Christ, Peter wants us to know that God is above all authorities. This means that Christians can still obey governmental authorities and yet be faithful.

Similar charges were made of Christians in Peter's time and Augustine's time. Both were charged with disrupting the social order and tranquility of society. This is the same charge that is lodged against Christians in former communist societies and also within Muslim cultures.

Question 5. In several different ways Peter affirms the identity of Christians. Formerly they were merely Gentiles, now they are the people of God. Jews historically understood that they were different from the cultures around them because of their unique history and laws. For Gentiles who were becoming Christians this sense of unique peoplehood was and is a difficult concept. When we, as Christians, understand our unique and distinct identity in the world, there is a freedom not to conform. If we do not expect to be different, then we think that there is something wrong with us when in fact we are just being who God called us to be.

Question 6. In the postmodern free world, Christians are often accused of being close-minded, inhibitors of progress because they do not see all desires and actions as equally acceptable. Christians are also accused of close-mindedness because of their claim that Jesus alone is Lord and the only way of salvation for a fallen world.

Question 7. The behavior of television evangelists Jim Bakker and Jimmy Swaggart in the 1980s had a widespread impact on how inconsistent behavior affects non-Christians' perceptions of the gospel. Of course not only televangelists but pastors and others also bring the gospel into disrepute when they act in ungodly and immoral ways.

Question 10. Recent surveys reveal that there is virtually no distinction between how believers and nonbelievers handle moral issues. In the first several centuries of the church most instruction for new believers was on how Christians were to act. The expectation was that right belief would follow right behavior. In contrast, a great deal of current Christian instruction revolves around what Christians should believe and how they should deal with personal, emotional problems. There is very little instruction on how Christians are to behave.

If this guide is being used for small groups, be sensitive about probing. This is a very personal question and the level of group trust will determine how much someone can risk in answering the question.

Question 11. There are many ways to answer this question. From housing homeless people to tutoring neighborhood children, Christians today are involved in many acts of care and compassion. With just a little historical research it is possible to document that education, health services and food distribution for the poor have been generated by Christians. Through the ages Christians that have treated the poor with great dignity and brought much good to society.

Study Five. The Two Cities. Hebrews 11:8-16.
Purpose: To discover the important power of hope.

Question 1. Many people in your group will have lived in several cities. Encourage them to mention them by name and discuss what they liked and disliked about each.

Question 3. *Peace,* as Augustine uses it, means the sense of social order that provides a unifying center for a society. The Hebrew word *shalom* is often translated as *peace.* A better translation is "social order and harmony."

Question 4. Many Christians today have an individualistic view of the Christian faith that looks only for personal salvation. The idea of the "city of God" looks more at the shared and social dimensions of salvation. The city of God has provided rich insights on how Christians should approach participating in the social and political activities of their culture. The concept of the city of God was the foundation for the idea of a Christian civilization that dominated the Middle Ages—the vision of all of humanity living together in social, political and economic harmony under the lordship of Christ.

Question 6. Abraham's uprooting his family is an expression of faith that God will keep his promise. As he moves into the Promised Land he is expressing hope that there is a better life for his family in the future.

Question 7. While they did not have an earthly hope, they did have a heavenly hope; that is, they were expecting something beyond that which was normal and natural, something beyond this world.

Question 8. The resurrection of Jesus is the ultimate foundation of Christian hope for life beyond this world. Because he has been raised we can look forward with anticipation to both joining him in heaven and seeing him return to restore the earth. Other acts of God in Scripture, from the exodus of Israel from Egypt to the miracles of Jesus and the prophets, can inspire us to hope. In addition, our own personal experiences of God's work in our lives can be signs and pointers to God's future.

Question 9. In light of this passage we can say that the Promised Land is a provisional land. Perhaps the old gospel song captures this provisional nature for Abraham and his family, and for us: "This world is not my home, I am just passing through."

Question 10. God's work in this world always has a present and a future dimension. Perhaps we could say that God's promises are tantalizing tastes of a future banquet. God never wants us to be satisfied and settled in this world, and he calls us to look forward to his coming kingdom.

Question 11. Hope is one of the most powerful forces in human life. For a sports team that has no hope for the playoffs, the season becomes terrible drudgery. A student that has no hope for graduation finds it difficult to study. In contrast, when there is hope for the playoffs, the intensity of play increases. When graduation is in sight, all one's courses are taken with focused energy.

Question 12. Most of us will have lots of experiences with city life. Not all of it will be good, of course. But for the sake of this question, select the best you can think of about living together in an urban context, and then reflect on how heaven might be an improvement and enrichment on that which you treasure most.

Study Six. The City of God. Revelation 21:1-8.
Purpose: To consider what life will be like in eternity.
Question 1. Augustine points out that the sense of continuation and duration in this current existence is different in kind from the experience of everlasting life in heaven. This is a good place to discuss the difference between eternal life as a new quality of existence versus a duration of existence. Duration of existence means that we would continue to live forever in the state we now find ourselves. Only a moment's reflection is needed to show that few would volunteer for such a possibility. Who would want to continue forever with the limitations of present existence—whether it is physical, emotional or relational? Eternal life means a change in us in which there is freedom from sin and every inclination of evil.
Question 2. The ultimate freedom of the city of God is to be freed from sin, our own innate personal compulsion to do wrong.

The pursuit of freedom has been one of the foundational aspirations of modern culture. The Pilgrims came to America to pursue freedom of worship. Later, the desire for economic and political freedom led to the declaration of independence from England. In Europe, the cry for liberty and equality drove the French Revolution. In the twentieth century this pursuit has meant freedom from moral restraints or any family restraints or even genetically determined gender restraints. As the modern worldview continues to deconstruct around the pursuit of freedom, Christians have the opportunity to point to a different kind of freedom—that which finds its center in God and leads to a shared submission and freedom from evil.
Question 3. The seventh day of creation, the day of God's rest, becomes the ultimate rest for humans as well. In an age in which there is either exhaustion from compulsive overwork or boredom from overstimulation, the experience of satisfying, refreshing rest touches us deeply.

There also is a unity between the first and last pages of Scripture concerning human dignity. Satan encouraged Adam and Eve to grasp for their dignity in rebellion against God. The sad result is human depravity and estrangement from God. At the end of Scripture, in the book of Revelation, dignity is a gracious gift which God delights to bestow on those who live before him in humility. Augustine says it so well: in the city of God we are given "the dignity by participation that could never be gained by desertion."

Question 4. This is an overview question. Don't explore any answer in-depth at this point, just look for as many attributes of the new creation as you and your group can discover.

Question 5. In many ways the tension of the Christian life springs from the tension inherent in the newness of God in our lives mixed in with our old selves in the midst of an unrenewed creation. The dynamics of a renewed creation are prophetically and poetically described in Isaiah 65:17-25.

Question 6. A home together; an enduring covenant; an intimate bond; a partnership.

Question 7. "Dwelling," "tabernacle" and "home" are ways that this verse could be translated. Each captures something rich and fresh about what is happening here. A dwelling is a place where one takes up residence. "Home" captures the emotional tone of the passage. "Tabernacle" in the Old Testament was the place where God dwelt among Israel and received their worship. Another question that might be interesting to pursue, if you choose to take the time, concerns Jesus Christ: Jesus is called Immanuel ("God with us") by the angel prior to his birth. How is the presence of God in the new heaven and earth different from Jesus' presence among his people now?

Question 10. This question allows for you and the group to consider the unity of Scripture. Genesis begins with the presence of God, which is lost by sin, and Revelation ends with the presence of God, which is restored by grace.

Question 11. In an age that does not like to make moral distinctions, Revelation 21:8 is a sobering verse. God's grace does not do away with the exercise of his justice or judgment.

Question 12. This question should generate some lively discussion. Keep in mind that while paradoxes challenge us to think and ponder, we don't have to be able to explain or understand a paradox for it to be true.

Sources

Study One
Augustine, *Confessions* 1.1, trans. R. S. Pine-Coffin (New York: Penguin, 1961), p. 21.

Study Two
Confessions 1.5, p. 24.
Confessions 2.1, p. 43.

Study Three
Confessions 8.12, pp. 177-79.

Study Four
Augustine, *The City of God* 1.36, ed. Vernon J. Bourke, trans. Gerald G. Walsh et al. (New York: Doubleday, 1958), p. 64.
City of God 2.3, pp. 68-69.

Study Five
City of God 11.1, p. 205.
City of God 14.1, p. 295.

Study Six
City of God 22.1, p. 507.
City of God 22.30, pp. 542-43.

Further Reading

Augustine. *Christian Instruction; Admonition and Grace; The Christian Combat; Faith, Hope and Charity.* Fathers of the Church, vol. 4. New York: Cima Publishing, 1947.

———. *The City of God: Books I-VII.* Fathers of the Church, vol. 8. New York: Fathers of the Church, Inc., 1950.

———. *The City of God: Books VIII-XVI.* Fathers of the Church, vol. 14. New York: Fathers of the Church, Inc., 1952.

———. *City of God: Books XVII-XXII.* Fathers of the Church, vol. 24. New York: Fathers of the Church, Inc., 1954.

———. *The City of God in Seven Volumes.* Loeb Classical Library. Cambridge, Mass.: Harvard University Press; London: William Heineman, 1963-1972.

———. *Commentary on the Lord's Sermon on the Mount with Seventeen Related Sermons.* Fathers of the Church, vol. 11. New York: Fathers of the Church, Inc, 1951.

———. *Confessions.* Fathers of the Church, vol. 21. New York: Fathers of the Church, Inc., 1953.

———. *Confessions and Enchiridion.* Translated and edited by Albert C. Outler. Library of Christian Classics. Philadelphia: Westminster Press, 1955.

———. *The Happy Life, Answer to Skeptics, Divine Providence and the Problem of Evil, Soliloquies.* Fathers of the Church, vol. 1. New York: CIMA Publishing, 1948.

————. *The Immortality of the Soul, The Magnitude of the Soul, On Music, The Advantage of Believing, On Faith in Things Unseen.* Fathers of the Church, vol. 2. New York: CIMA Publishing, 1947.

————. *Letters (1-82).* Fathers of the Church, vol. 9. New York: Fathers of the Church, Inc., 1951.

————. *Letters (83-130).* Fathers of the Church, vol. 18. New York: Fathers of the Church, Inc., 1953.

————. *Letters (131-164).* Fathers of the Church, vol. 20. New York: Fathers of the Church, Inc., 1953.

————. *St. Augustine's Confessions in Two Volumes.* Translated by William Watts. Loeb Classical Library. 1631; reprint, Cambridge, Mass.: Harvard University Press; London: William Heineman, 1977.

————. *Sermons on the Liturgical Seasons.* Fathers of the Church, vol. 38. New York: Fathers of the Church, Inc., 1959.

————. *Treatises on Marriage and Other Subjects.* Fathers of the Church, vol. 27. New York: Fathers of the Church, Inc., 1955.

————. *Treatises on Various Subjects.* Fathers of the Church, vol. 16. New York: Fathers of the Church, Inc., 1952.

————. *The Trinity.* Fathers of the Church, vol. 45. New York: Catholic University of America Press, 1963.

————. *The Works of Saint Augustine: A Translation for the 21st Century.* Augustinian Heritage Institute. Hyde Park, N.Y.: New City Press, 1991-2001.

Bentley-Taylor, David. *Augustine: Wayward Genius.* Grand Rapids, Mich.: Baker, 1981.

Brown, Peter. *Augustine of Hippo: A Biography.* Berkeley and Los Angeles: University of California Press, 1969.

Chadwick, Henry. *Augustine.* Oxford and New York: Oxford University Press, 1986.

Lawless, George. *Augustine of Hippo and His Monastic Rule.* Oxford: Clarendon, 1987.

Scott, T. Kermit. *Augustine: His Thought in Context.* New York and Mahwah, N.J.: Paulist, 1995.

Thigpen, Paul, comp. *Restless 'Til We Rest in You: 60 Reflections from the Writings of St. Augustine.* The Saints Speak Today. Ann Arbor, Mich.: Servant, 1998.

VanderMeer, F. *Augustine the Bishop: The Life and Work of a Father of the Church.* Translated by Brian Battershaw and G. R. Lamb. London and New York: Sheed & Ward, 1961.